Flouriish.online

To the womxn who are healing! We dedicate our book to the phenomenal womxn in our lives. Linda Williams, Sonja Pritchett, Mamie Pritchett, and Gloria Kaymore.

Efflorescence

(flowers): the action or process of developing and unfolding as if coming into <u>BLOSSOMING</u>

(flowers): an instance of such development

(flowers): the fullness of manifestation: <u>CULMINATION</u>

Mission

Our mission is to help womxn thrive unapologetically in vulnerability, self-love, and revolutionary self-care as they learn to master the art of healing while basking in excellence and nourishing in growth. We will provide products and services to assist every womxn on their journey to become their best selves.

Flouriish Efflorescence Introduction

Welcome

As womxn, we have been socialized to put the needs of others above our own. We want all womxn to know it's okay to put yourself first and place value on the way you care for yourself. Each month, you will have a theme and a Soul Care mission to complete. The Soul Care activities will allow you to pour into yourself as you learn, unlearn, and relearn parts of who you are. You will see a significant component in each Soul Care mission is the five senses (sight, sound, smell, taste, and touch). The five senses will allow you to intentionally be mindful of how sensory practices can contribute to your emotional well-being. We encourage you to Flourish through reflection as you complete each Soul Care mission.

Importance of Self-Reflection

Along with our Soul Care missions, Bloom Themes are assigned to emphasize a specific growth area every month. Each month's Bloom Theme will end with four reflective questions. Reflection is vital for growth and maturity. To bloom unapologetically, we must identify behaviors and actions that are both beneficial and detrimental to our healing journey. Thinking helps identify specific behavioral patterns. By recognizing these patterns, we can avoid harmful behaviors and replace them with healthy alternatives.

Healing Playlist

Music also plays a pivotal role in the healing journey. It can reduce stress, expand creativity, treat depression, stimulate brain waves, and release "the feel-good" chemical, known as dopamine, into your body. We were hoping you could create a healing playlist of songs that reflects your healing journey. Your playlist will include ten songs, the title of the songs, and the artist. This playlist can be used as you work through your Soul Care missions.

Flower Healing

Flower themes are assigned to each month to highlight the unique healing components that help the mind, body, and spirit. The vibrant colors, distinctive petals, and uniqueness of each flower have the power to heal wounds as we bloom on our self-healing journey. Flowers go through a transformative process as they grow, bloom, and wither. As you expand on your journey, water your roots, extend through the dirt, and give yourself the care and light you need to flourish.

My Efflorescence Hope

On this page, you will write down a list of things you desire to Flouriish on your efflorescence journey.

Ex:

I hope to build a stronger sense of confidence in my abilities.

I hope to heal from the trauma I never shared with anyone.

I hope to create a pattern of more positive self-thought.

January
Gratitude

Gratitude is the key to life; It is what makes the difference between hope and hopelessness. Gratitude can travel through time, transforming our past pain into future growth. Our happiness needs to choose to be grateful in all things. As wonderful and positive as life events can be, negative occurrences have the power to mold us into the person we are today. Being grateful for both types of instances helps us to create our narrative. Gratitude challenges us to think more creatively and more deeply about life and its meaning. Gratitude is a great way to recognize just how far we've come. Our outlook on life is the divide between the glass being half empty and being thankful that we have a glass to fill. Each day is better when we change our perspective. Gratitude adds sweetness to the bitterness and the learning of your lesson.

Trollius flowers, also known as the Globe Flower, represent gratitude. A "Golden Queen" Trollius flower is known for loving direct sunlight and being a fast grower. Like the Golden Queen, we may catch some harsh weather but be able to withstand it and develop because of it proudly. Our beauty shines vibrantly when we are grateful for each moment that grows us. Bloom unapologetically in gratitude.

Quote: "Gratitude clears the view in blurry situations making empowerment and growth evident." **- Tyra Kaymore-**

Flouriish Soul Care Mission (Taste): Every Little Step I Take
Make or buy your favorite meal and as you are eating, try to identify each ingredient. Reflect on how many steps are needed to create this dish. Think about how different experiences and events in your life came together to create

the person you are now. Much like the process of making your meal, your personal experiences have aided in your overall development. Only by encountering these unique experiences will you become this better version of yourself.

Set a Date: _____

Reflection Questions
1.When thinking about the processes and events that made you who you are, did you emphasize more initially happy or initially sad events? Why?
2.What did you learn from these events?
3.Who do you believe you are now because of it?
4.What are you grateful for today?

Root
"Cultivate your thoughts"

Tye's Healing Playlist: Toast x Koffee
Bri's Healing Playlist: Be Alright x Evan & Eris ft. Steven Malcolm

What are the three things you are grateful for?

February
Bravery

Bravery is a form of strength and growth. There is going to be a season of hardships, challenges, and uncertainty. Remember, inside your garden box to overcome these seasons, and you have the mentalities to face these challenges boldly. Apply for your dream job. Get that degree. Purchase that house. Book a session with a therapist. Walk away from toxic relationships. Start over. Let your bravery shine through your doubts.

King Protea represents change, courage, and transformation. The name stems from the flower's resemblance to a crown. The Protea has one of the largest families in the garden, with over 1,500 variations ranging from shrubs, tall trees, and sugar bushes. Much like the King Protea, we are multifaceted beings of royalty, just like a crown. Bloom unapologetically in bravery.

Quote: "Each petal tells a different story of what you have overcome. With love and light bloom into a beautiful flower" -**Brianna Elum-**

Flouriish Soul Care Mission (Touch): *Plucking Petals*
Start by gathering three assorted flowers that you like. After collecting the flowers, you grab a bowl or container and fill it with water. Remove the petals from the flowers and, with each touch of the petals, make a releasing statement (i.e., "I release the fear of failure.") before dropping them into the water. It is only by releasing our worries and taking chances that we genuinely exercise bravery.

Set a Date: _____

Reflection Questions

1.How did you determine what obstacles you would associate with each petal?

2.What are the challenges you experience with being brave?

3.How will you practice bravery this month?

4.How did you feel after releasing your fears?

Sprout

"Cultivate Your Thoughts"

Tye's Healing Playlist: Brave x Jhené Aiko
Bri's Healing Playlist: Authors of Forever x Alicia Keys

1. In what ways have you been brave today?

March
Intentionality

Intention begins with what motivates and drives us. It breaks actions down into purpose and gives the "why" behind the "what." Passions are the things that inspire us, something we invest our time and efforts in, and things that require no reward. They are things that we do because we enjoy doing them. The reason something is being done is almost as important as the action itself. Our intentions have the power to affect our commitment and consistency when following through with our decisions. They help create a pattern of on-brand progression toward your goals, developing the habit of making decisions based on the bigger picture. Intentions will also guide us away from choices that are not in favor of the person we wish to become and the things we want to accomplish. Intentionality is life's compass that keeps us on the path of our choosing. It helps designate what we will do next versus what happens to us. Our intentions help push us to accomplish our goals and must be revisited to refresh and regain focus behind our vision.

Orange roses represent passion and energy. Before the 20th century, orange roses did not exist. Researchers began experimenting with red and yellow Roses to give new and unique variations to the already famous and beloved flower. By focusing on the same goal, researchers provided a new appearance and meaning to a rose. Similarly, we use our intentions to guide us to a greater purpose and brand-new achievements. Bloom unapologetically in intentionality.

Quote: "Your intentions are a direct connection between where you are and where you are going. Having a strong sense of purpose can motivate oceans of change."
- **Tyra Kaymore-**

Flouriish Soul Care Mission (Sight):
Stemming From Intention

Draw a tree to represent your primary goals in life. For each branch, write a word that motivates you toward that goal. For example, if my goal is to buy a house, I would put on some of the branches "have a place of my own, become the first homeowner in my family, have more creative workspace." Once you draw out your initial motives, continue to elaborate on each goal. Take "become the first homeowner in my family," my branch-offs could be "making my parents proud, creating a new legacy within my family, challenging myself to make larger investments." After you are done, take a moment to look at your tree and see how much intentionality plays in your decision making.

Set a date: _____

Reflection Questions
1. After finishing your Stemming From Intention, did you notice a trend in what you're motivated by? What inspires you the most? Is it family, a lifestyle, a feeling?
2. When did these intentions form for you?
3. Why are these things important to you?
4. What actions did you take this month to intentionally further your goals?

Nourish
"Cultivate Your Thoughts"

Tye's Healing Playlist: All for Us x Labrinth & Zendaya
Bri's Healing Playlist: Believe In You x Raja Kumari

1.What intentions have you set for the week?

April
Authenticity

Stand tall and take a look in the mirror. We are a unique blend of inherited magic that makes us the author of our own life. An essential aspect of being authentic is knowing and owning the narrative of your story. On the journey to becoming, ignite the inner fire to find your passion, own who you are, and blossom into your unique flower. It's time to place seeds in your garden that are a true reflection of yourself and weed out the narratives that others have projected onto you. In the world, someone is craving for us to show up with our unique talents and gifts. Remove the mask and let the authentic you show. When you are your most authentic self, you can attract valuable relationships.

The Platycodon flower represents endless love and honesty. It is the only flower with balloon buds that bloom into a star shape. Platycodon comes in purple, blue, pink, and white. This flower does not try to be like other flowers; its purpose is to bloom like a star. Much like the Platycodon, we all have unique ways that we stand out. Bloom Unapologetically in authenticity.

Quote: "Shine bright as you work on becoming you authentically." **- Brianna Elum-**

Flouriish Soul Care Mission (Smell):
Unmasked Truth
Whisk together 1 tbsp of coconut oil, 2 tbsp of raw sugar, and five drops of honey in a small bowl until all ingredients are well blended. To add a beautiful smell,

stir in your favorite fruit or five drops of essential oil (some great oils to use are lavender, lemon, eucalyptus, and spearmint. Adjust ingredients based on preference). After mixing the ingredients, take a deep breath, and inhale the scents from the mask. Gently place the mask inside your hand and put it on your face for 15 minutes. Use a wet cloth and wash off the mask. Much like the mask's removal process, you will wash off the narrative's others have projected onto you.

Set a date: _____

Reflection Questions
1.Cleansing is a purification process that allows you to wash away actions and people that no longer serve you. After washing off the mask, what did you feel like you were washing away?
2. At what age did you begin to develop false narratives?
3. What emotions arose as you combined the different scents?
4. Write down three things that make you unique?

Forming
"Cultivate Your Thoughts"

Tye's Healing Playlist: I Believe x DJ Khaled ft. Demi Lovato
Bri's Healing Playlist: I Like That x Janelle Monáe

     1. Write down three ways you display your most authentic self.

<u>May</u>

Growthify

" Growthify" stems from self-confidence in our ability to progress; It is mindfulness of our limitless potential. We set goals for ourselves, but these goals are no limitations. We, as individuals, are ever-evolving, so are our goals. The perspective we have of our own lives affect our potential. Growthify challenges us to think outside of our current abilities to understand that wisdom and knowledge are both infinite. Because we can learn what we have the potential to do is more far-reaching than we could ever imagine. Things take time, they take steps of progress, but the amount of progress can be never-ending. Push ourselves to dream bigger, plan more thoroughly, and do more work.

Lilacs represent renewal and confidence. They bloom several times throughout the year. Some varieties of Lilac bushes can survive in temperatures as low as -60oF. This flower continues to demonstrate strength in multiple seasons and remains in a constant state of advancement. This flower does not go about doubting it's potential but grows in its purpose no matter the conditions. Much like the lilac, we are resilient, and our growth will be unhindered in every state of life. Bloom unapologetically in your growth.

Quote: "Your potential can stretch across the universe or just across the street. It all depends on your mindset." **- Tyra Kaymore-**

Flouriish Soul Care Mission (Sound): _Explore Your Roots_

Take time to research your origin story. Reach out to friends and family members who have known you over lengthy periods. Have them share with you their earliest and favorite memories of you. Think about what you didn't know during that time and compare them to what you know now. Let this motivate you in your growth journey and see your potential increase.

Set a Date: _____

Reflection Questions

1. What was your favorite origin story, and who was it told by?
2. Were any of these memories shared? Were there parts that you remembered that the storyteller had forgotten? How often?
3. What did you learn about yourself from these stories?
4. What memories are being formed right now that reflects your growth?

Flowering

"Cultivate Your Thoughts"

Tye's Healing Playlist: Now or Never x Kendrick Lamar ft. Mary J Blige
Bri's Healing Playlist: One Step At A Time x Jordin Sparks

1. Write down three areas of potential growth.

June
Forgiveness

Forgiveness is an ongoing mission. It breaks a negative connection that has been made, and sometimes the bond has grown strong. Sometimes forgiveness takes place between multiple people, and sometimes it is an internal disconnect within oneself. Forgiveness tears apart broken bonds and replace them with strong new connections. Based on a deliberate decision to release ourselves from anger and pain. It does not require changed actions or apologies. Forgiveness does not excuse the actions of others but is a requirement for our healing journey. We must think outside of the person who wronged us and desires our growth above all. Our journey of forgiveness takes different forms. It is an internal decision, so it does not always require verbal communication.

White Tulips represent forgiveness, purity, and serenity. Tulips also signify worthiness and new beginnings. Tulips were once more valuable than most people's homes. In the 1600s, they cost almost ten times as much as an average-class worker's yearly salary. Much like the Tulip, forgiveness is extremely valuable to our healing journey. It is necessary to have a fresh start in healing from situations. Bloom unapologetically in forgiveness.

Quote: "Forgiveness is an unlimited source of power to continuously free ourselves of hostility." **-Tyra Kaymore-**

Flouriish Soul Care Mission (Touch): _The Color of Your Emotions_

With your favorite paint, take a white sheet of paper and finger paint to express your feelings about a situation that requires forgiveness. Allow your fingers to feel the paint and perceive it as the emotions you feel. With every touch, leave the negativity on the page and allow forgiveness to create something new.

Set a Date: _____

Reflection Questions

1. What was the most significant thing you've forgiven someone for?
2. How did you feel while writing about it? Were you angry, disappointed, relieved?
3. How often do you think the average person apologizes? This includes both small and large offenses, as little as cutting someone off in conversation or bumping into someone you did not see.

Blossoming

"Cultivate Your Thoughts"

Tye's Healing Playlist: Sandcastles x Beyoncé Knowles
Bri's Healing Playlist: Forgive Me x Chloe & Halle

1. What are three things you want to forgive yourself for?

July
Joy

Joy is the feeling you experience that radiates from within. Joy is a highlighted emotion that brings an everlasting presence when you are engaging in things you love. Allow yourself to tap into joyful moments fully. Joy is giving yourself self-compassion as you heal from certain things more than once. When you pour Joy into your heart, that same joy and happiness radiate onto others.

The Bird of Paradise represents joyfulness, paradise, anticipation, and excitement. While the paradise bird is known for its three bright orange petals and three dark blue petals, they can also be found in the color white. The positioning of the petals mimics the appearance of a tropical bird in flight. Like the soaring petals from the Bird of Paradise, spread your arms open as you reach for joy. Bloom unapologetically in joy.

Quote: "Create moments of joy that nourishes your soul."-**Brianna Elum**-

Flouriish Soul Care Mission (Taste): Hold Me By The Heart
Get dressed and put on your favorite outfit. It's time for you to take yourself on a solo dinner date to your favorite restaurant. When selecting the location for your date, pick a place that brings your heart joy. After the solo date, reflect on what made your heart smile with joy during the date?

Set a Date: _____

Reflection Questions

1. How did it feel to intentionally carve out time to take yourself on a solo date? Were you nervous or excited when you arrived?
2. What is something new you discovered about yourself on your date? How will you apply what you learned about yourself to cultivate joy in your life?
3. How did you decide on the location for your solo date?
4. Congratulations on your solo date! Write down three things that brought you joy about your meal?

Sunlight
"Cultivate Your Thoughts"

Tye's Healing Playlist: Optimistic x Sounds of Blackness

Bri's Healing Playlist: You Bring Me Joy x Anita Baker

1. Name three ways you experienced joy this week.

August
Visionary

A visionary is authentic, transparent, true to their values, and holds steadfast to their hopes, goals, dreams, and aspirations. Visionaries boldly plan for the future while simultaneously modeling vulnerability, unlearning damaging behavior, and inspire others to act. Visionaries are intentionally planted, and their goals are "specific", "measurable", "attainable", "relevant", and "time-bound". Their goals, dreams, hopes, and aspirations help feed their vision as they sprout roots to encourage others to act. Bloom unapologetically with vision.

Sunflowers represent foresight and creativity. The color of petals is associated with success and confidence. The radiant Sunflower exudes warmth and inspiration. The yellow petals contribute to Sunflower's ability to stimulate the brain's logical part, inspiring thought, and curiosity. Stand tall like a sunflower with confidence as you shed light on your ideas. Bloom unapologetically with vision.

Quote: "When I dare to be powerful, to use my strength in the service of my vision, then it becomes less and less important whether I am afraid." - **Audre Lorde-**

Flouriish Soul Care Mission (Sight): Shining With Passion
Draw a pair of sunglasses. Inside the sunglasses' frames, write down four goals, you are excited about accomplishing this year. On the days you get discouraged and want to give up on your dreams, grab

your sunglasses, and shift your lens to refocus on your vision.

Set a Date: _____

Reflection Questions
1. What steps will you take to obtain the goals written inside your sunglasses?
2. What parameters are you putting in place to ensure you are achieving your goals?
3. What is the time frame you plan to accomplish your goals?
4. What barriers do anticipate encountering as you work on accomplishing your goals?

Blooming
"Cultivate Your Thoughts"

Tye's Healing Playlist: Story by Stevie Wonder x Big Sean

Bri's Healing Playlist: Big x Pastor Mike Jr.

1. What is one way you will pour into your vision?

September
Innovation

Innovation is an extension of creativity and need. Innovation requires dedicated time to think analytically regarding your current state and your goals. It is an in-depth look at how best to proceed to the next level in your life. Innovating requires taking knowledge of the past and the anticipation and wisdom of what is to come. It requires tact, ingenuity, imagination, originality, and vision. We all can innovate, but it takes courage to try something new and different. Your next move can be your best move yet.

Marigolds represent creativity. Gardeners often use them because they act as a natural repellent to pests. Marigolds also have several different healing properties because they contain anti-viral, anti-bacterial, anti-fungal, and anti-inflammatory properties. Marigold flowers contain lutein, a substance beneficial to the human eye. Marigolds are historically believed to be magical because of all of their healing properties. In our healing journey, we must find various ways to stir up our magic and utilize our numerous gifts. Bloom unapologetically in innovation.

Quote: "There is no recipe, there is no one way to do things — there is only your way. And if you can recognize that in yourself and accept and appreciate that in others, you can make magic." **-Ara Katz-**

Set a Date: _____

Flouriish Soul Care Mission (Taste): *Rewriting the Script*

What's your favorite meal? Think of a new way to recreate it by transforming it into a dessert, brunch, or dinner option instead. What are some new ways to update and transform your creation? Try out the new recipe and reflect on the outcome.

Reflection Questions

1.How many variations of your favorite meal did you come up with? Did you seek help for your recreations (i.e., internet search, asking a friend, etc.)?

2.How did your new meals turn out? What succeeded? Which ones failed?

3.How did you feel when trying out the new meals? Were you confident or nervous?

4.What challenges did you face when forming new ways to approach the recipes? What did you learn from these challenges, and how can you apply this to your ideas and innovation?

Pruning

"Cultivate Your Thoughts"

Tye's Healing Playlist: EAT x Tobe Nwigwe & Fat
Bri's Healing Playlist: Bigger x Beyoncé Knowles

1. List three different methods to achieve one
    particular goal. (Plan A, Plan B, and Plan C)

October
Vulnerability

Vulnerability is always a decision. We have the choice to reveal our most authentic selves, our most honest intentions, our greatest desires, and our deepest thoughts. It puts ourselves at risk of being understood for who we truly are and deciding whether or not to accept what we see. Vulnerability is permitting ourselves to be exactly who we are and allowing space for others to do the same. This trait is interactive. We must create a safe space within ourselves for openness and confidence. Vulnerability is the place where intimacy and self-love are created. Being vulnerable is what validates the true relationship with ourselves and others. Aspects of exposure can sometimes be uncomfortable, so it is up to us to press into the discomfort to create a strong sense of self and meaningful bonds with others.

The Lily symbolizes vulnerability. The "lily of the valley" flower represents humility and purity, which are necessary for vulnerability. Oil from these flowers has softening agents that aid in skincare. Our vulnerability journey requires us to soften our hearts and tough exteriors to grow our individuality and self-love. Bloom unapologetically in vulnerability.

Quote: "Vulnerability is having the courage to show the world your most secret self."
- Tyra Kaymore-

Flouriish Soul Care Mission (Sound): Guess Who?

Write a list of 4 words that you believe best describe you. Reach out to your closest friends. Ask them to list off four words that best describe you as a person. Actively listen to the feedback of your loved ones without a rebuttal. Reflect on the lists they give you and compare them to your original list. Think of ways you can best outwardly show your inner traits. It can also help if you reach out to a friend to hold you accountable for demonstrating your desired characteristics.

Reflection Questions
1.What are you most ashamed of, and What are you Embarrassed about?
2.How did you feel writing about it?
3.Who are the people in your life that know your secrets? What about them sets them apart from others?
4.What steps can you take to create safe spaces for yourself and others?

Watering
"Cultivate Your Thoughts"

Tye's Healing Playlist: Smother Me x Olivia Nelson
Bri's Healing Playlist: Confidently Lost x Sabrina Claudio

1. Write one thing about the future that you are anxious about.

November
Healing

Healing is a multifaceted process that ebbs and flows; It is not all sunshine and positivity. Healing is deep soul work that requires us to look in the mirror, address our trauma, and remove the mask. There are days where you will feel empowered and days where you will feel uncertain, and that's okay. It's admitting to your faults; it's practicing humility. As you work on healing, you have to make a conscious effort to unlearn and relearn on the journey. Take the damaged parts of your story and turn it into divine beauty. Pour into yourself and nourish your soul as you heal from everything you are carrying.

The Lotus Flower represents enlightenment, self-regeneration, and rebirth. The growth process of a lotus is rooted in murky waters away from the sunlight. Just like the lotus flower, we have the capabilities to rise from dark moments as we swim through murky waters of hurt, trauma, hardships, and destress as we bloom into our best selves. Bloom unapologetically in healing.

Quote: "The healing process is like a sea that ebbs and flows. Sometimes the waves are filled with rifts while other moments are filled with calmness. Give yourself grace as you calm your healing storm."**-Brianna Elum-**

Flouriish Soul Care Mission (Smell): *Lotus Flower Bomb*
Take a trip to your favorite candle store or local store that sells aromatherapy items. When you arrive at the

store, identify three scents that represent love, happiness, and peace. After the end of your scent journey, purchase the smell that resonated with you the most.

Set a Date: _____

Reflection Questions
What did you enjoy most about picking your favorite scent?
How did you narrow down which scent you would purchase?
What emotion did you pick to go along with your scent, and why?
If you could use one word associated with your experience for happiness, love, and peace, what would you use? How did you feel yourself change when smelling different scents?

Growing
"Cultivate Your Thoughts"

Tye's Healing Playlist: Healing x Arlissa

Bri's Healing Playlist: Heavy x Kiana Ledé

1. List two areas of your life that require healing.

December
Wholeness

Wholeness is an ever-evolving process. It's a journey that focuses on exploring the unmasked truth of your inner self. The completeness trip requires us to dig deep into our soul and discover places, things, and experiences that our heart has been afraid to acknowledge. As we dig into the garden of wholeness, we begin to see past hurt, trauma, and brokenness. We hope you pour into your planted seed by honoring your wholeness amidst the pain. When we embrace our fullness, we invite others to do the same. Understand that wholeness does not equate to perfectionism; instead, it's about finding harmony and becoming one with ourselves.

The Gladiolus flower represents the strength of character, integrity, and faithfulness. Gladiolus sprout in pink, purple, red, yellow, green, and orange. Its sword-like shape is named after the Latin word "gladius," meaning sword. Bloom unapologetically in wholeness.

Quote: "You need the rain, sun, weed eater, and soil to bloom in wholeness." -**Brianna Elum-**

Flouriish Soul Care Mission (Sound):
Blooming with Compassion
Let's take time to speak to our inner self with compassion. This activity will require you to look in the mirror and complete the following sentences. I am allowed to_____, I love that I _____, and I can do better at holding space for myself by _____.

Set a Date: _____

Reflection Questions
Sun: How do you continue to learn and relearn yourself?
Rain: In what ways are you pouring into yourself?
Soil: How do you make peace with your past?
Trimming: List specific people, places, and things that detract from your wholeness. How will you set boundaries in your life, so they don't resprout?

Flouriishing
"Cultivate Your Thoughts"

Tye's Healing Playlist: Good Thing x Zedd & Kehlani

Bri's Healing Playlist: Good As Hell x Lizzo

1. Name one thing that made you feel whole this week.

Flouriish Until Letter

Flouriish Until is a statement of continuation. Efflorescence is a never-ending journey of self-discovery and improvement. Life is full of unpredictable, which requires each element from each month. Knowing how and when to use the right combinations can be complicated. Be patient with yourself and others along your journey. We all are discovering new things about ourselves we go, so we each require grace. Flowers, in all their beauty, go through different seasons where they are pruned, plucked, even come close to being destroyed. These plants' lives were not promised to be easy, but they bloom gloriously and bring life to others with the right care. Flowers are not just used for their beauty, but they heal, provide nourishment, purify the air around them, and provide livelihoods for entire ecosystems. The life they bring is far-reaching beyond where they are planted. Challenge yourself to improve to the utmost parts of your being from the deepest depths of your soul. Flouriish until eternity.

Brianna Elum and Tyra Kaymore

Lightning Source UK Ltd.
Milton Keynes UK
UKHW021851171220
375389UK00012B/103/J

9 781087 908762